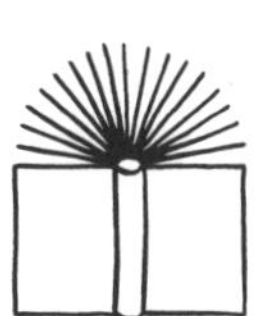

Clare Goodwin
Dennis and Denise

Texts by

J. Emil Sennewald
Rebecca Geldard
Tony Grisoni
Frances Loeffler
Aoife Rosenmeyer
Chris Fite-Wassilak
Clare Goodwin

Nieves

Clare Goodwin
Dennis and Denise

First Edition

Published by Nieves
www.nievesbooks.com

Kindly supported by Kanton Zürich and
Erna und Curt Burgauer Stiftung

ISBN 978-3-905999-95-2

Contents

Tony Grisoni is a British screenwriter and filmmaker living in London, Rebecca Geldard is a British writer and art critic based in Wales, Chris Fite-Wassilak is an American writer and art critic living in London, Frances Loeffler is a British writer and curator based in Canada, Aoife Rosenmeyer is an Irish writer, art critic and translator based in Zürich and J. Emil Sennewald is a German art critic, writer and philosophy teacher based in Paris. Clare Goodwin is a British artist and curator living in Zürich.

Clare
or, who's afraid of stripes and stories, most abstractively?
J. Emil Sennewald

'The gradient is a net we throw out to sea,
without knowing what we will haul back in it.'
Maurice Merleau-Ponty *Eye and Mind*, 1962

The moment I started writing this introduction I reached out to one of Clare's catalogues – suddenly holding the spine, wondering. By chance, I found the book on the top of a pile of magazines. A copy of *'A'A'* magazine lay underneath the catalogue, its cover upside down. This flip meant that the stripes reproduced on that cover matched perfectly with those on Clare's catalogue. Happy coincidence? *'A'A'*s special issue was about the work of famous Venezuelan constructivist or concrete artist Carlos Cruz-Diez – a fresh ninety-fiver whom I met several weeks ago in his Parisian studio and curator of a group exhibition I had seen at Espace de l'Art Concret / Donation Albers-Honegger near Nice, using Gottfried Honegger's collection. In 2008, this art centre was a starting point for my growing interest in geometric abstraction. I had to recognise the wit of its contemporary followers, especially in Romandy, called eventually by the curators Christian Besson et Julien Fronsacq 'extended abstraction'.

The reason I am telling this story as an introduction to Clare's anthology of stories, made in response to one of her paintings, seems obvious: one could easily catalogue her work in the heritage of geometrical abstraction, suggested by the motifs she uses – as induced by the accidental superimposition of her catalogue and the art magazine. To understand if this suggestion correlates with her artworks, and if this art-historical approach allows us to experience the phenomenological dimension of her paintings, let us look into this coincidence a little more.

Through the works of artists such as Philippe Decrauzat, Stéphane Dafflon or Francis Baudevin, abstract painting has drifted into a kind of meta-painting. Unlike their ancestors, such as Carlos Cruz-Diez, who tried to 'change our perception of the world and thus the world itself by art', the new generation (the three mentioned above are all born between 1964 and 1974, coeval to Clare) appears concerned with the hypnotic, optical qualities of geometric motifs. Decrauzat, for example, borrowed the carpeting pattern of the famous boy-on-tricycle-scene in Kubrick's *The Shining* for an abstract painting. One must know that Kubrick, using the uncanny effect of subliminal perception, changed the carpet's pattern between cuts. Decrauzat's appropriation of this motif frames the 'perception changing'-effect of geometric patterns, using the eye-blink shift to provide a sense of critical distance from which to consider aesthetically induced manipulation.

Clare's works also employ this 'trick'. Browsing through her œuvre brings up some funny, yet serious appropriations, sometimes with site-specific performances: her artist-led curatorial project 'The Museum of the Unwanted', critical confrontations with heroes of art history such as Nam June Paik in 'Un-plugged', or her series of kitchen paintings titled with names like *Margaret*, 2008, *John*, 2007, *Grace*, 2007 or *Nigel and Trish*, 2009. One might find similarities with suggested narratives where there are none – or 'just' geometrical patterns, as in the work of Dafflon. One might also identify a deep and intelligent reflection on the ubiquity of geometrical structures in everyday life, a symbolic grid giving us the warm and confident feeling of being in cartesian control of our surroundings at all times.

All this would offer a neat interpretation of Clare's art in the continuity of art history, nobilising her painting in a similar way to the mainly male tradition of geometric abstraction. It would be, if it weren't for those names: Heather and John, Alice and Dave or Dennis and Denise. With them comes this unconscious, but palpable, feeling that their experience is pointing beyond painting, abstraction, and the concrete. In fact, meeting her tableaux is like stumbling into an old acquaintance, but one we have never met before.

This 'constructive nostalgia' as she titled her 2016 show in Centre PasquArt in Biel, reveals a kind of souvenir in the sense of Jean-Luc Nancy pointing out the supportive or standby meaning of this word.[1] It reminds, not in the sense of bringing back, but in constructing what it might be possible to recognise and thus be 'lived' today. As the Constructivist's impact on our way of thinking has served to switch us back to modernity any time we experience the aesthetic impact of abstraction in the everyday, Clare's 'painting scenes' effectively hook us onto the line of history, not to drag us back into the past, but take us forward.

Through stripes and shadows we are projected into a leaky world of remembrances. The colours used eerily allude to the presence of curious company, recalling, for example, George's and Martha's interweavings in *Who's Afraid of Virginia Woolf?*. For they, too, provide that good but unsettling feeling of what it is to be wrapped in the grid of geometrical patterns, to be in what Maurice Merleau-Ponty called: 'the Nessus' tunic of the world'– it fits perfectly, yet stings like hell.

That's what writing is all about. And that's what Clare's paintings provide as an experience: a sense of becoming aware of the net's grip thus wandering, half dreamy, half laughing, into what will become a story, our world. You are going to read some of them and be triggered, or better, decide to dwell in the spaces they create.[2]

[1] Jean-Luc Nancy, Je me souviens…, 24.03.2017, www.diaphanes.net/blog/je-me-souviens-jean-luc-nancy-4485, May 25, 2018

[2] As for me, I am continuing to meditate about the stripe's chance and art critics' lives by gazing on an old photograph of Octave Mirbeau, one hell of an art critic. Very famous and well paid in his time, great writer and automobile-enthusiast he is posing self-reliant behind his Victorian desk in a neat bourgeois interior, holding his head, museful, with his left hand, while the right is dynamically posed on the chair's armrest. Above the horizontal bar of a mighty moustache, the art critics' gaze stares back at the camera. While I am trying to escape his piercing glance, I become aware of the grid, holding the figure in place. The wallpaper's vertical stripes are joining the ones on his trousers, coating this writer on the brink of modern abstraction, already in the net of perception he is going to knit through his texts. Around one hundred years later, I will meet the modern mindset of Octave's interior design on the walls reproduced by Hergé's editor on the second and third page of TinTin's album covers. Again, 20 years' later, Baudevin will put the alternating vertical stripes in clear blue and dark blue as real wallpaper on the walls of the gallery space, quoting Haddock's headquarter by the title "Moulinsart". And until I am projected in a nostalgic maelstrom of childish comic-fascination and early art experience, I reflect the kinship of image and writing – suddenly holding the eye, wondering.

Glass Houses
Rebecca Geldard

She has rolled off her tights and they sit like a sad tan-coloured pool of skin on a patch of balding grass. Unworn they were one thing, but the evident history of wear – the deflated sense of a missing limb, and the effects of bodily pressure and sweat on fine mesh – makes them appear more narrative construct than object. They remind her of a crime scene, an ex-boyfriend's pet lizard and the congealed effect of heated milk – the little wrinkle when you touch the surface, like a tiny tin of paint left without a lid.

It's hardly Ballard territory, this is Bermondsey, but the modest, predominantly glass high-rise affords its occupants the kind of view that might lead them to believe they are directors of, not actors in, the production of another day in the life of London. Until they scramble out onto the street, perhaps. Or, until the sky's eyelid closes, the lights come on and it is their turn to perform on the other side of the pane, unwittingly or not, as one of a vast ensemble cast in a play of perfunctory gestures. From a distance, you can imagine swiping a finger across the night and flicking through each diorama, pinching and unpinching the action for more detail of the lives inside.

The air in the communal garden is not what you'd call fresh, it's too close to the high-rise's bins. But after a 15-hour shift indoors attending to others, this time – any time – outside and under the sun is golden. She pulls up her tunic dress to expose a pair of uncooked thighs, a pale offering to Helios. When it's not blocking the light, the building opposite creates enough glare to laser a retina, but she's too tired to move inside and find her sunglasses. She hates that darkening effect that happens when you go indoors after time in the sun. Everything appears muted like reruns of old output from LWT, all russet reds, airforce blues and ochres where the primaries should have been. It feels like the onset of a brain injury, or what happens to her laptop screen when it's running out of power, as if her life's battery is draining down before her eyes.

In the theatre of windows, on the sixth floor, a man is looking out. He can't be seen from outside, there is too much light bouncing off the glass. If you were looking up at his building from the street, there is a chance you might notice a darker patch where he stands, stationary, in a pixelated sky. Even with the aircon on full, it is as hot as a greenhouse inside his flat, a place of order, cleanliness and devoid of all non-essential personal effects. Visitors might imagine he has good storage, but there are no things to hide away, he has no room in his home or his head for the past. Nostalgia, like an alien visitor to an inhospitable planet, would wither and die should it ever have reason to land here.

Closing her eyes, the nurse lets her knees fall to one side and spreads her arms out on the parched ground. The smell of grass, even this poor excuse for turf, always takes her back to a time-worn but unsulliable place of joy. Her grandparents' garden. She loved the unbearable heat of the greenhouse in the summer, and the smells, standing in the gulley between the sentry lines of tomatoes and runner beans for as long as she could bear the humidity. She allows herself to drift here, hover in a world where the most pressing decision was which flavour of Mini Milk to buy at the village shop. In the semi-conscious half-life of a daydream there was less chance of falling too far. It was possible to snorkel across the top of your memories, feel the cold patches of deeper water underneath but fin quickly out of them into places pre-warmed by the sun.

They call him unkind things at work, in emails he hasn't been cc'd on, and in last year's company yearbook he was described as "The guy most likely to … go postal" beneath a picture that appeared to corroborate this as a possibility. He has one of those faces that always appears to be resting between expressions, in transit from thought to thought. It's a face that's hard to remember and befits his role as a kingmaker, a curator of other people's lives. The Minecraft matrix of terraced housing below looks like a still from a coffee-table photography book. On a small, greenish swatch a woman in a dishevelled state lies legs akimbo surrounded by bits of clothing. He can't decide if she is dead or just very relaxed, or which of these possible scenarios he is more envious of; to have been taken out of the game, or to be out for the count.

Dennis and Denise
Tony Grisoni

– *Oh Denis doo be do*
I'm in love with you, Denis doo be do
I'm in love with you, Denis doo be do
I'm in love with you

– What can I get you, sir?

What I want is an espresso with a splash of cold milk. (Can't you have a normal coffee like everybody else?)

– Just a coffee.
– Americano?
– Espresso
– You got it.
– Put a splash of cold milk in there, would you?

– Hot or cold?
– Cold.

So clever.

– Shiamese vodka!

Get it? Got it. And we all did. Bonded, so cheap. Harry Palmer. Beef-A-Roni. In a supermarket.

– Champignons... It's not just the label. These do have a better flavour.
– You're quite the gourmet, aren't you?

This was in the dark city. I knew the outside daylight was fake - the rain streaming the windows was down to special fx.

– You know what? This little room takes me back to my parents' house.
– Yeah?
– That wallpaper, those chairs, the shelves and those ornaments. Even the stag horns somehow.
– Cool.
– Not cool. You called a spade a spade back then. There wouldn't have been that Schiele print either.
– The picture?
– They'd never have a thing like that on the living room wall. Or anywhere else.
– I guess...
– Those curtains too. We had the same ones.
– I like them.
– Yeah? Do you?

What would his brains look like on them?

– They're cool. Here's your coffee. Sir. Enough milk? Anything else?

It's going to be him or me. I'll have a Pink squirrel.

But better calm down. I don't want to leave. Not just now. It's dark, getting darker. He's watching me. He knows. They're closing. He smiles - gives a little wave.

The night falls with a turn of the corner. Now this is real. Real night. I know it down here - this labyrinth of streets, fluorescent tubes starring the darkness, stalls selling giant snails and plastic hairbrushes, batik and dead fish. Moving hands and strange tongues and looks. Eyes on my every move. I know this place.

I spill a man's cup of tea. Bumped into him accidentally. I am at a tea stall. I apologise but he doesn't accept the apology. He demands another cup of tea. I see how big he is. I quickly replace it. But that isn't enough. He isn't placated. He wants NODRUM MEAT.

– Get me that Nodrum Meat!

Nodrum Meat? I don't know what that is.

It's a kind of bush meat. I asked someone. He explained. He said you had to boil bush beef for hours. It's a very long and complicated process. Like an aquatic centipede? "Overpoweringly delicious and nauseating." Trimalchio's Supper. Is that what this is? An invitation to dinner?

I go in search of the Nodrum Meat - threading through the night market labyrinth.

I am back with the man who is even angrier and more aggressive. I put my foot down - make it clear - I've had enough of his demands. The words never leave my throat. He lurches towards me with - murderously insane. My heart thumps. He grins.
– Oh yeah, I heard it alright. I heard your little heart go bang.

I am back on the hopeless quest. I find a rundown café that is about to close. They have sold out of most things. The owner comes over, wanting to be helpful. He's Australian, so has heard of the dish I'm hunting for. But I notice him quietly checking with the waitress. He's asking her what the meat is and how to prepare it. He's stringing me along. Then I realise - he's drunk. He starts the process of making the Nodrum Meat. He has no idea what he is doing. It's going to take a long time. I'm regretting asking him. But I can't return to the man empty-handed.

While the boiling is going on I drift away. What shall I do? Wander the streets at night, hoping to wake? There is a swift sea-change in the atmosphere. I am hijacked. Car bonnets start opening automatically - synchronously. The driverless cars reverse out. More and more of them. In formation. A ballet. A grand finale. And not my story at all.

He felt the sun, hot on his neck. Strange, at night. Perhaps he'd burned himself the previous day, perhaps an insect had bitten him. He woke in a night sweat. He lay there panting, not daring to move. He could feel animal heat on his back, hot breath on his neck. The man was lying behind him, he knew. He passed the night like that - rigid with fear, eyes staring, waiting for the dawn. He thought:

– I could lose my life.

What's in a name?
Frances Loeffler

In early summer 1972, he applied for the position of art critic on one of Britain's major broadsheets. This, he reasoned, would allow him to spend time in the U.K. in order to be near his English wife while she finished a teacher-training course at a college in West Sussex. They had recently married abroad, and this would be the first time they would spend a significant amount of time together in the same country. He got the job, packed a small suitcase, and made his way to Calais for the ferry. In the weeks leading up to the start of his contract he spent time at his wife's parents' house near Petworth. Afternoons were passed playing tennis on a sunken court at the back of the house or lying on the lawn talking about the latest books over tea. It was so far removed from the clandestine and risky exhibitions and reading sessions he'd held with friends in a one-room flat in the Eastern Bloc town that it felt unreal. The hammock by the fish pond, the apple orchard and horse paddock felt like a stage set, as though painted an artificial shade of dappled green. He felt like a character in a Chekhov play.

None of his wife's family and friends could pronounce his name. Translated into English it meant 'harvest', a rather lovely meaning that belied the everyday nature of what back home was the equivalent of 'John' or 'Peter'. Such poetic nuances were lost in this new setting. Instead, it was a red flag, a sore thumb that caused endless uncomfortable explanations and comical misunderstandings. Some were curious about the name, asking him where he was from. B-zh-een-h-sh-chy-k-veee. What were all those 'z' and 'k' and 'v' clotted together, and those weird accents over certain letters? Several people showed goodwill, valiantly having a go at getting the pronunciation right. But sometimes an introduction was followed by polite silence and a slight flicker of the eyelids. Were they associating his name with the headlines concerning his homeland and what had happened there?

One particularly painful incident involved an elderly relative who insisted on calling him after a type of food popular in his country. He laughed with the rest of them but quietly resolved to find a new name for himself. It would be an English name that would work like a camouflage, allowing him to go about unseen. He would decide on the name before he started the job in order to get off on the right foot with his new colleagues. His wife protested, feeling a pang of guilt at his readiness to slough off his old self in order to fit into her home. She loved his name. She thought it was beautiful, unlike anything she had heard before, the music of it, its sheer complexity. She was proud of her mastery of it. She had managed to bend her tongue to its rhythms and grooves where others struggled. She persevered with introducing him by his name, cajoling friends and family to wrap their tongue around the strange syllables, as though tasting a new food.

He didn't feel guilty about chucking in the old name. He had worked hard to put time and distance between himself and his old life, which seemed painful and grey now against the limey hues of the Sussex stage set. He didn't know it then but later this colour schema would switch. The image he had in his head of his home town would take on warmer tones, and he'd return there several times a year seeking out old friends. The problem he had was: which name? This proved more difficult than he had expected. He was aware of the nuances and attachments that surround names. He suggested a few that he liked to his wife only to have her explain that here they were deemed old-fashioned or laughable in some way. Worse still, some had double meanings that on explanation made him blush. Some were shared by people he knew and didn't like, rendering them unusable. His wife, inexplicably, couldn't abide any name beginning with 'J'.

He wondered if he should choose a literary name, something that would demonstrate how elevated and contemporary his tastes were despite his troubled nationality. A name from one of the Kingsley Amis or Philip Roth novels his wife's family had been discussing, for example. How about Micheldene? Portnoy? She thought not. On the weekend before he started his job he and his wife went to a gallery near the Angel Islington in London. There was an exhibition that had received good reviews in the press. The work was very of-the-moment. Very American. There were paintings showing strips of pure, bright colour. They made him think of the pantone colour charts that were all the rage that summer: grass green, avocado green, hot pink, lemon chrome, bright violet. They brought to mind a favourite dress of his mother's.

He noticed that there were no titles listed on the wall labels accompanying the work. Instead, the paintings were simply numbered in sequence.

He appreciated this, knowing the awkward baggage that can come with a name. The pursuit of a new name for himself was at the forefront of his mind. He wanted to get the matter settled, particularly as he was to start the new job on Monday. One painting was an exception: it had the title Beth. This was curious, he thought. Who was Beth? Had she been a lover, a friend? Or was the painting itsgelf a 'Beth', carrying the sort of qualities and characteristic that a 'Beth' might, and what were those? He pondered this for some time, sitting on the hard bench under the steady eyes of the guard. It was only later that he found out that Beth was the second letter of the Hebrew alphabet. The catalogue informed him that the artist had made a point of never titling his works. It was the artist's widow who had decided to name the painting as a matter of expediency only as the exhibition was being installed. She had assigned the numbers, too.

On the Monday morning he set out for the newspaper office, feeling anxious that he still hadn't found a name. The matter was becoming urgent. Why was this proving so difficult? Should it be Paul? Dexter? Steve, Mike, Don? As he cleared the last corner before reaching the steps to the office a bright red fire engine careened down the street towards him. In the moment that it flashed past he caught the name written in capital letters across the front. It made him think of Clos Saint-Denis, a vineyard in France he had visited once, and then of a French girl from long ago who had the female version of the name, Denise. Yes, Dennis would do. What's in a name, after all, he asked himself. He pressed the intercom. A few moments later, a crackling voice was asking him who he was.

Cuckoo

Aoife Rosenmeyer

The package is a cuckoo visible through the glass. Brown tape mummifies battered cardboard, sitting on a hard, off-white surface. Wait to find out if it will be released.

A few years before there had been another, which they sent after mother died. Cool damp had risen to assault the unprepared nose; it clung to a couple of books. It was a forgotten smell. Once disagreeable, it now meant what had been left behind. Not mouldering decay but preservation.

It's humid here too, but that moisture is blasted away by the assault of cold inside every door. Purifying substances are dispersed instead in the circulating air.

The materials they handle at the clinic are flexible and smooth to the touch. They are slightly fleshy and work like extensions of the user. A patient's brittle body, when touched to reconnect sensors or change pads, contrasts with the engineered stuff around them.

Sometimes there's talk as they do this; it has to run along the approved lines, though it rarely elicits a response and nobody seems to enjoy it. Cases who engage, and those whose families visit them, are elsewhere. Monitors relay how the system is designing the treatment. Sometimes they light up with a video call, but other screens are more attractive. Speaking is discouraged between the care technicians. There is not much to say and sounds have been designed to fill the silence.

Several years have passed operating in the same section. No surprise in the assignment, the process was clearly defined: recognised qualifications were matched to labour shortages. The specifics were still checked in the holding village and everyone's blood was screened. Poor results were the usual criteria for rejection. Others were isolated and then sent back during the quarantine period.

The places they inhabited looked foreign at first, though their featurelessness became familiar. Work and accommodation and places in-between share the same colours. There is a uniform in the clinic, which is removed and left there, and another one for transit.

This transport and accommodation disconnect the staff. Between work and the shuttle and the dormitory are moments of moist heat and glimpses of manicured plants that flower facing other people. Grit in the air that gets between the teeth is a strange relief from other textures. By now the possibility of other pleasures is abandoned. The food is an established ritual, exchanges are cursory. Each person becomes ever more detached. Personal belongings are hidden; they may not even exist.

Letters and messages went back and forth before. Then they became routine, pointless. There was nothing and too much to say. On each side they grew more distant. Disinfecting fluids dissolved their ties. The package will not be released but destroyed. It is a threat to the environment.

Dear Dennis
Chris Fite-Wassilak

As we were walking out of the station yesterday, a woman was crouched by the railings. She had a sign at her feet that said, 'I am embarrassed, but I need help.' We'd just gotten off a train full of chanting football supporters – drunk, elated, full of the kinship of winning. Or maybe the desire for that kinship, where they expect it to be infectious and that you might join in on their swaying bleats. We smiled, mostly to ourselves, and also mostly to keep them at bay and pre-empt any conversation to try and gauge our enthusiasm for their team, or their sport, or whatever. And then released out into vacuum of the open, and the woman is bent over there, crying. And I knew where my sense of comradeship actually lay. And still we just kept walking.

This is just a preamble to say:

I've used up all my shit. As you well know.

This isn't so much my patience running out, as it is simply just a point where I no longer register, no longer feel able to give a shit to lift a finger. I've been peeled and I've been pelt. And while it's no big melodramatic disaster, just the dam-holding feeling is one I can't keep with. Or, I say that and it's been years of it anyway, and could be years more, but maybe this letter is just my own illusion of a feeling being that might be, or should be, infectious.

We've been going to food court in the mall nearby, and just sitting among the punters, while I marvel at their determination. To sit, to eat, to make a choice among the fluorescentocopia. I was about to write 'without thinking about it', but then who knows. But still to just do, shamelessly, with apparent disregard for the interminable muzak buzzing from the speakers ten metres above their heads, for the terrazzo flooring alternated with woodprint lino, for the 5-ply plywood chairs they sit in. And yet there I am saying 'they' as the uniform plural, as the capital one body one mind rule, and somehow the mall brings me each time to that point, and then to catch myself at it. I use it as a chance to imagine each body dissolving into thousands of rays of some kind of glowing matter, sprawling through the floor and the atria, eventually merging into a larger light. The walls melt away, perhaps playing ruefully with the open sky. When an energy ball meets an energy ball coming through the wry.

One of the kids sat near us at one point was trying to pick a fight with this girl. Telling her to shut up. She turned around quick as a thumbtack and started going on about her uncle, so-and-so Adams, so he better shut up. After she glides on, kid tries to regain his posture, flairs off to his friend: 'You know the Adams family? They're an old old family, used to be around here but they ain't around no more. For her to be sayin that is brave, brave.' Shrugs, 'She don't know me, she don't know who I am, what I done.'

Fair enough, I thought. One way to invoke that staircase spirit, a comeback – downsizing her whole family tree – when she's already long gone. Brave indeed. How would anyone know who you are, what you've done? The mall was giving all this a kicking soundtrack of some lo-fi mini folk-symphony cover version of a 90s pop song. Takes a minute to recognise the ditty, and you end up thinking it's somehow more timeless than it is; but it gave their elongated exchange a sort of picaresque quality, that there might be some tussle and averted eyes but it was all going to turn out alright.

Just passing through: the mall is the new demesne, I think, the latest incarnation of feudally parcelled land with permitted temporary trespassers, dependent entirely on monetary exchange. I like to think I'm bunking the system when I sit there, picking at the layers like a courageous scab, but then of course we always get hungry after half an hour don't we?

Which reminds me, I still haven't made that mix tape of cover to cover versions, starting with Dylan's Baby Blue, to Van's Them version of it, to that Beck song that uses the riff, and on to Beck's own mariachi version in Spanish of the song. I guess the trail ends there, and then to start another circuit? Maybe with Kraftwerk and Afrika Bambaataa and then that Rage's version of Renegades of Funk. I just imagine a public space serenaded with such half-cover versions and echoes, a swirling void of mirrored songs that people would unwittingly get sucked into. Humming snatches of songs all day, without knowing which fragment they got stuck with. Or all of them. The Demise of the Song, that would be a good mix title.

I'm tip-toeing around the edge again. The point of this was resolution, or at least resolve, and again and again I'm falling back into dissolution. When all the things point towards edges fading, asserting a distinction between things that all of a sudden feels against a grain. It's not even a desire, it's just blunt…fact? Is that even a word anymore? It just is. And what you is is ain't.

You remember that woman we saw for a bit back just after university, and how she would always go on about her best friend – that they were exactly the same personality, that they were so similar that it had led to trouble in the past. The trepidation of then meeting her when they came to visit, wondering if there'd be some sort of mirror confusion, that we might instead fall for them. And then turns out all she meant by 'trouble' was that she'd started sleeping with her boyfriend, as if that was some sort of existential fault of the clueless friend. And of course the friend was totally – not unrelated, but just her own person. I think you just thought she'd be hotter. But who knows what people are looking for, where they see reflections, what they're looking to dissolve themselves into.

I'm gonna have to give up on the dissolution. So, I guess this is a letter of resignation. Demanding that you, finally, just resign. Step back and let me just take the wheel. You can see what it's like to be the passenger for a while, even just fall asleep. Grow a beard, muse about writing that graphic novel and not playing the harmonica, grow old and get dementia, I don't know. If the denial wasn't mutual, I'd ask you to stop denying me this. So I'll stop denying myself. Please.

Your other/better/half

D.

Afterword (Text Collage Part 2, Facebook 2017)
Clare Goodwin

Love you too babes
Have you seen this Dennis lol
February is going well
What a catalyst you turned out to be
Got my 10cc head on lol
For all you bikers out there
Morning babes
Morning darling
Cheese on toast on the go with Worcestershiresauce, delish
I'm on the brandy, well it makes you randy doesn't it lol
I'm proud of my Irish Catholic heritage and don't give a fuck what anyone thinks, aahh I'm

drunk I'm drunk you silly old cunt, as drunk as drunk can be...

Blitzed my kitchen, flash bleached everywhere, you can eat your dinner off me surfaces

Stuck in traffic, anyone know what's wrong?

Yay driving home for Xmas

I can spot a shop lifter a mile away they always have a back pack and look well dodgy!!!

Watching whatever happened to Baby Jane, bloody brilliant

Kids get too much today, spoilt, ungrateful shits!!!

Cracks me up

My poor Dennis having a mare of a day won't finish work until 2pm, can't wait to have you home for Xmas

Into the Valley, peas sure sound divine lol

Brings back memories of my sisters Birthday party, someone bought her this, and me, mom, dad and bro went out and left her to it, bloody hell, place was trashed lol

Who can tell me which annoying song kept this absolute classic from the top spot

Looks like my little ones off school again tomorrow

Please stop putting this homeless shit on, ring this number etc, hostels are full to bursting, if you want to help donate old duvets, blankets, flasks full of tea/coffee etc

Fucking footballers on bench with hot water bottles, talk about being pampered, that's why I don't go to footie matches anymore, if they can't be arsed to turn up then why should I, I'm fucking done with it!

Morning my love